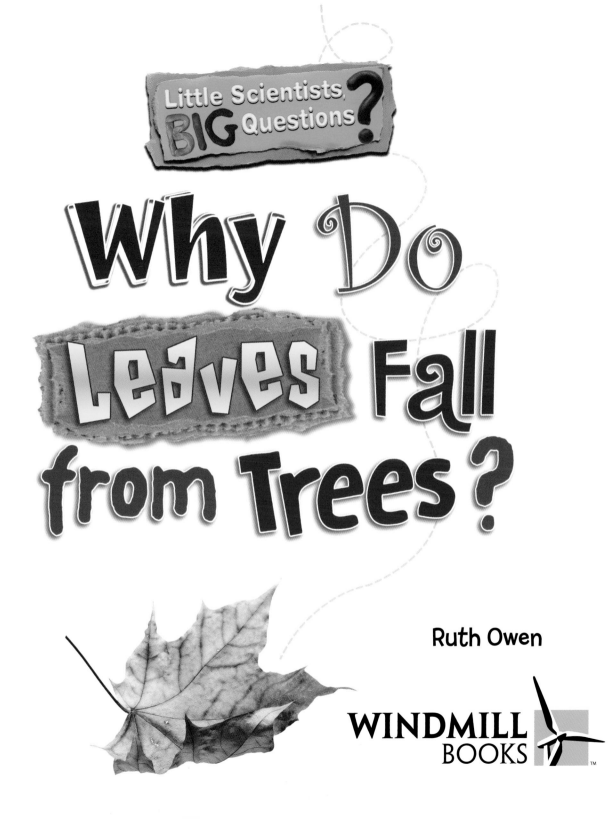

Little Scientists, BIG Questions?

Why Do Leaves Fall from Trees?

Ruth Owen

WINDMILL BOOKS

Published in 2020 by **Windmill Books**,
an imprint of Rosen Publishing
29 East 21st Street, New York, NY 10010

Concept development: Ruby Tuesday Books Ltd

Author: Ruth Owen
Consultant: Sally Morgan
Designer: Emma Randall
Editor: Mark J. Sachner
Production: John Lingham

Image Credits:
Nature Picture Library: 11 (bottom left); Shutterstock: Cover, 2—3,
4—5, 6—7, 8—9, 10, 12—13, 14—15, 16—17, 18—19, 20—21, 22—23, 24.

Ruby Tuesday Books has made every attempt to contact
the copyright holder.

Cataloging-in-Publication Data

Names: Owen, Ruth.
Title: Why do leaves fall from trees? / Ruth Owen.
Description: New York : Windmill Books, 2019. | Series: Little
scientists, big questions
Identifiers: ISBN 9781725393523 (pbk.) | ISBN 9781725393547
(library bound) | ISBN 9781725393530 (6 pack)
Subjects: LCSH: Leaves--Color--Juvenile literature. | Fall
foliage--Juvenile literature. | Autumn--Juvenile literature. |
Seasons--Juvenile literature.Classification: LCC QK649.O8456
2019 | DDC 581.4'8--dc23

Manufactured in the United States of America

CPSIA Compliance Information: Batch #BS19WM:

For Further Information contact Rosen Publishing, New York, New York at 1-800-237-9932

It's autumn!

Why do green leaves change color in autumn?

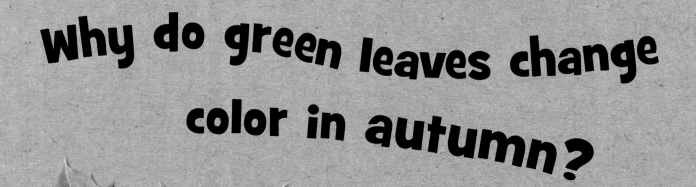

green

yellow

orange

red

brown

A tree's leafy story begins in **spring**.

The **sun** shines and the days get **warmer**.

Drip Drip Drop

There are lots of rain showers, too.

6

The tree sucks up rainwater from the ground with its roots.

Little green buds shoot from its bare branches.

roots

bud

The tree is growing new green leaves.

Soon the tree's branches are covered with thousands of leaves.

The leaves have a very important job to do.

8

Just like you, a tree needs **food** so it can grow **bigger** and be **healthy**.

How does the tree get food?

The leaves make it!

Get ready for some **BIG** science!

A leaf needs **3** ingredients to make food.

1 Sunlight

2 Water

Water flows from a tree's roots, up its trunk, along its branches, and into its leaves.

The water flows along these tiny veins.

3 Carbon dioxide

Carbon dioxide is a gas that's all around us in the air. You can't see it, but it's there.

stomata

microscope

A leaf takes in carbon dioxide through tiny holes called stomata.

The holes are too small to see without a microscope.

More BIG science coming up!

A leaf makes green stuff called chlorophyll.

Let's say it!
"CHLOR-uh-fill"

It's the chlorophyll that gives a leaf its green color.

sunlight

The chlorophyll in a leaf traps sunlight.

It uses the sunlight to turn water and carbon dioxide into a sugary food for the tree.

water

carbon dioxide

As a leaf makes food, it also makes the oxygen that you breathe.

All **summer** the tree makes **food** inside its **leaves.**

The weather is becoming cool and windy.

The days are getting shorter.

Autumn is nearly here.

When autumn comes, a tree must get ready for the tough months of winter.

Why is winter difficult for trees?

There is not enough sunlight for the leaves to make food.

Often it rains less in the winter, so it's difficult for a tree to get water.

Water in the ground may freeze and become ice.

It's time for the tree to rest and save its energy.

The **tree** removes the **green** chlorophyll from its leaves.

Now its other **colors** can be seen.

These **colors** are normally **hidden**.

When spring comes, the tree will make chlorophyll again.

The leaves **stop** making **food**.

One by **one** they **die** and **drop** to the **ground**.

What happens to the dead leaves?

sssshhhhhh

A hedgehog has made a cozy nest of leaves under the tree.

She goes to sleep until the spring.

Zzzzzzzzzzzzzzz

18

Hundreds of **worms** live in the **soil** beneath the **tree**.

wood louse

We like to munch on dead leaves, too!

The **worms** like to eat dead **leaves**.

19

All through the winter
the tree rests.

But not all trees drop
their leaves and rest
in winter.

evergreen
tree

Evergreen trees drop some leaves and then regrow some all year round.

These tough trees keep on making food, even in winter.

Some evergreen trees have long, thin leaves that look like needles.

21

The sun is shining.

Drip Drip Drop

There are lots of rain showers.

It's spring again!

Little **green buds** shoot from the tree's bare branches.

The tree is growing **new** green leaves to make food.

The tree's long winter rest is over.

Now we know why leaves fall from trees.

Good work, little scientists!

My Science Words

bud
A tiny new growth on a plant that becomes a flower or leaf.

carbon dioxide
An invisible gas in the air. As you breathe, you breathe out carbon dioxide.

chlorophyll
A green substance made by plants that they use for making food.

stomata
Tiny holes on a leaf that open and close, a little like tiny mouths.